COMMUNICATING
IN A
SCIENTIFIC AGE

COMMUNICATING THE GOSPEL IN A SCIENTIFIC AGE

The Barclay Lectures 1988

HUGH MONTEFIORE

THE SAINT ANDREW PRESS
EDINBURGH

First published in 1988 by
THE SAINT ANDREW PRESS
121 George Street, Edinburgh EH2 4YN

Copyright © 1988 Hugh Montefiore

ISBN 0 7152 0631 1

Montefiore, Hugh, *1920–*
  Communicating the Gospel in a scientific
  age.
  1. Christian doctrine related to science
  I. Title
  261.5'5

  ISBN 0–7152–0631–1

This book is set in 11/12 pt Times

Printed by Bell & Bain Ltd., Glasgow

CONTENTS

*The Publisher acknowledges
financial assistance from
The Drummond Trust towards the
publication of this volume.*

FOREWORD

It was in November 1978 that the inaugural Barclay Lectures were delivered—by David Sheppard. The subsequent lecturers have been Robin Barbour, Gerald Priestland, George Thomas, Colin Morris and John Churchill.

The Barclay Lectureship had its origin in a tribute organised to mark William Barclay's retirement from his New Testament professorial chair in 1974. Part of this tribute was a Testimonial Fund to which contributions came from all over the world from people of all walks of life who wished to honour a man reckoned by many then and by many still to be the finest New Testament expositor of his day. It was this Testimonial Fund that was used to create and to maintain the "Barclay Lectureship in Communication of the Christian Gospel". It is a memorial to his outstanding work in the field of Gospel communication as teacher, preacher, writer and broadcaster.

1988 marks the tenth anniversary of the first Barclay lectures and also the tenth anniversary of William Barclay's death earlier in 1978. My fellow trustees and I were delighted when Bishop

Montefiore accepted our invitation to be the Barclay Lecturer in this anniversary year. Hugh Montefiore is a distinguished communicator in his own right and William Barclay himself would undoubtedly have approved of our choice. We commend this publication of the manuscript of his lectures to the wide public they richly deserve.

James Martin,
Chairman of the Barclay Lectureship Trustees

PREFACE

I make no pretence of being a scientist: in fact I was educated in the classics. However, when I was a Fellow of Gonville and Caius College, Cambridge, I was fortunate enough to rub shoulders with many eminent scientists, and the relationship of religion and the sciences has fascinated me ever since. And so when I was invited to give these lectures on the William Barclay Foundation in Glasgow on *Communicating the Gospel in a Scientific Age,* I gladly accepted. They are printed here as they are to be delivered on 1st, 2nd and 3rd November 1988.

Hugh Montefiore

1

THE GOSPEL IN AN AGE OF SCIENCE

It is an honour to be invited to give the William Barclay Lectures on the Communication of the Gospel. I had the pleasure of meeting Professor Barclay on two occasions, both of them in Cambridge. On the first, he had just finished a session with a New Testament panel of translators for the New English Bible. If that was not an exercise in communicating the Gospel, I don't know what is, for you can't communicate the Gospel until first you know precisely what you are talking about. The second occasion was when he accepted an invitation to preach at the student service at Great St. Mary's, the University Church, when I was Vicar. I can see him still today in my mind's eye, his not inconsiderable figure leaning over the pulpit, his face lit up with a smile, as he rammed home some gospel point with a joke that would be likely to make it stick with an undergraduate audience. That too was an exercise in the communication of the Gospel. It was in the Sixties, and now we are twenty years further on. I am glad to honour a great Christian man, and I hope that the memory of him will long flourish.

"Jesus Christ is the same yesterday, and today and tomorrow." That is true, but our understanding and interpretation of Jesus must be in terms of the language and symbols which make sense to us today. We so often forget that biblical phrases, which may perhaps 'turn us on' if we have been brought up within the Church, may mean little or nothing to the great majority of our fellow men and women. We have to put the everlasting Gospel into words which will make sense to the minds and convict the hearts of people near the end of the twentieth century.

There is another striking difference between our days and those when the Gospel was first preached. We live now in a very secular age. Very many people pass most of their lives without acknowledging God or even thinking about him. We sometimes forget that in New Testament times everyone believed in God—the question was what kind of god or gods you believed in. That has been true down the centuries, and indeed it is still true in most of the world today. It is only in Europe, and especially in Northern Europe, that more and more people either deny the fact of God's existence, or are sceptical about it; or they accept that he exists, but lead their lives as though he did not.

This attitude radically alters the whole question of communication of the Gospel. For the Gospel is about God; God who created the universe; God who is behind the great pageant of evolution, beginning with the Big Bang, and continuing through billions of years, with billions and billions of galaxies, and even more billions of stars, until man evolved on Planet Earth a very short time ago compared with these aeons of cosmological time. And since human beings have only the haziest idea about who has brought them into being, God disclosed himself in a special way to the Jewish people, and this self-revelation culminated in a personal self-disclosure in Jesus Christ.

His coming is Good News, because he not only showed us both how to live and what God is like in terms of human personality, but he also enables us to be ourselves. He renews us, by enabling us to accept ourselves, even though we know that we are, each one of us, unacceptable; and we are able to accept ourselves because we know that God himself has accepted us, and we know that because we see on the Cross of Christ how much God loves us and cares for us. If God Incarnate has, as it were, gone to those lengths for us men and for our salvation, then this gives us renewed faith and hope and love. For when we turn afresh to God in the faith of Jesus Christ, we find that God himself dwells in our hearts through his Holy Spirit which we share with others within the fellowship of believers. This fellowship we call the Church. His grace is always with us and the new life which he gives us makes life without him seem more like death. This new life is a foretaste of life with him for ever throughout eternity.

This is the essence of the Gospel. I am sure that each Christian adds to this his own personal interpretation from his own reading of the Scriptures and as a result of his Christian experience and understanding. But the heart of the Gospel is about what God has done for us through Christ; and so, if a person does not believe in God, he cannot accept the Gospel. And this is what very many people seem to find so hard in these islands today—to believe in the living God. It is no good starting with Christ if people do not believe in God. It is like talking to a person in English when they cannot understand the language: there is no communication. You cannot communicate the Gospel on the supposition that Jesus was just a good and worthy man, you end up with humanism, You cannot concentrate simply on Jesus of Nazareth and forget about God, because Jesus always pointed away from himself to his Heavenly Father, and unless we do that too, we end up with Jesus worship, and that is not Christianity.

Why have we become such a secular country that we find belief in God so hard nowadays? There is no easy answer to this question, but the main reason is that we live in an age whose chief characteristics are advances in scientific knowledge, and the application of this knowledge in modern technology.

As a result of technology we can now achieve through our own efforts many things which used to be thought to be in God's hands. Nowadays we do not pray for rain, we seed the clouds with chemicals instead. When a person is ill, we don't just anoint him and pray for him, we send for the doctor and use medication or surgery. This is very different from biblical times, when drought or illness was thought to show God's displeasure. It is technology, not faith, that now enables us literally to move mountains. We can begin the process of human life in a test tube. We can create energy from the nuclear elements of matter. We can know what is happening anywhere in the world, and even see it on our television screens as it happens. We are well on the way to creating Artificial Intelligence. In doing these things we are using the intelligence and power given us by God, but it seems to many that modern technology makes God remote from their consciousness.

We should not be able to achieve these technological feats if it were not for spectacular advances in our scientific knowledge. Many people think that the sciences have also proved that God does not exist, or have at least shown his existence to be highly problematical. This, of course, is not the case at all, and few scientists today imagine that it is. But it is a view popularly held, and has been held for a long time. Professor Colson drew attention to Bishop Butler, who in the eighteenth century wrote in the preface of his *Analogy of Religion*: "It is come, I know not how, to be taken for granted by many persons, that Christianity is not so much as a matter for enquiry; but that it is now at length taken to be fictitious."[1] The same assumption about religion has been made in the Communist world, where so called 'scientific lectures' have been given in order to eradicate religion—in fact with little or no effect.

Old-fashioned views tend to die hard in public consciousness. Schoolmasters are apt to reflect ideas they learnt a generation ago. Journalists are largely ignorant about the relation between religion and science. And so there exists in the public mind a vague idea that religion is now out of date. People may still believe in God in their own private lives, almost as a kind of hobby. Religion has become, if you like, a minority interest, rather than the publicly accepted basis of life. This situation is very far removed from the biblical revelation of the living God, the Creator of the universe, who reigns sovereign in his creation, and who judges evil and who acts to inaugurate his Kingdom on earth. And so there is, in a scientific age, comparatively little communication of the Gospel, because the Good News of the Kingdom so often falls on ears which have been largely deafened to its message.

1. C. A. Coulson, *Science and Christian Belief*, (O.U.P., 1955), p.9.

How can the ears be unstopped, and communication restored? There are three crucial avenues of approach. One is the personal testimony of individuals whose hearts and minds have experienced the touch of God and whose lives are lived in the consciousness of his presence. The second is to persuade people actually to read the Scriptures for themselves. I know that these need interpretation, but much of them, especially the Gospels, speak for themselves, and through reading them the power and the reality of God can break through. And the third approach is to show people, in an age of science, that science is not against religion, but on the contrary the sciences actually help us to understand the work of God within his universe. It is this third avenue with which I am particularly concerned in these lectures on *Communicating the Gospel in a Scientific Age.*

If we want to investigate the relationship of the natural sciences and religion, we must look at the origins of the sciences. In fact they were born in Christian Europe only a few centuries ago. The ancient Babylonians made accurate observations of the stars; the ancient Egyptians mastered the art of building huge temples; the Indians developed and advanced civilisation; the Chinese made great advances of technology far ahead of the Western world; the ancient Greeks were intelligent and observant and made some brilliant scientific discoveries— one has only to think of Archimedes and his bath. Yet under none of these did the natural sciences flourish.

What was it about Christian Europe that encouraged the natural sciences? Professor Tom Torrance has shown the importance for the sciences of some key Christian convictions about the nature of God.[2] "God

2. T. F. Torrance, *Divine and Contingent Order,* (O.U.P., 1981), p. 66.

is Light'': God, who is himself uncreated Light, bathes the universe with created light so that it is everywhere intelligible and accessible to knowledge. "God is good", so that the universe is not hostile, malevolent, or alien to the human spirit, and so it may be investigated without fear of the consequences. "God is faithful", so that there is nothing arbitrary or anomalous about the operation of the universe. As Professor Torrance wrote: "Orderliness and temporality, regularity and novelty were married together". The world is not regarded as 'necessary being', but as contingent, that is to say, subject to conditions, and these conditions therefore await scientific exploration.

The origins of the sciences have been investigated by others. Professor Jaki, a distinguished Hungarian Benedictine priest, who is also a well known physicist, has enquired into this matter in great depth.[3] He has pointed out that the sciences could not prosper under the belief, commonly held in the East and in the ancient world, that matter is evil or illusory, or that time is cyclic so that history repeats itself; viewpoints which lead to despair. He was shown how the way forward was being prepared by the early fathers of the Church and by the Church in the Middle Ages. The Muslim world, for all its wealth of culture, could not really encourage the sciences because of its overemphasis on the Q'ran and its view of God as too transcendent to take a real interest in his world.

It may be too much to argue that the rise of the natural sciences was inevitable within the Judaeo—Christian tradition, but clearly there are good reasons why it took place there. It is worth remembering that under the

3. S. L. Jaki, *Science and Creation*, (Scottish Academic Press, 1974).

Charter of our British Royal Society, its members were required to direct their studies "to the glory of God and the advantage of the human race." It would be strange if that which our religion has actively encouraged should turn out to be its implacable foe. In fact a lot of hostility has been caused through specific issues where the findings of the natural sciences seem to be directly opposed to the testimony of the Scriptures. I shall not deal with these now, as they come within the purview of the next lecture on "The Gospel and the Sciences".

It is my conviction that, properly understood, the sciences, far from being hostile to religion, actually require it. The sciences are based on regularities of nature, but why should nature contain regularities, unless they had been so ordered by God? The sciences investigate the nature and operation of material substances which we now know are, in their most basic forms, interchangeable with energy. But why should there be any matter or energy, unless it were created by God? I know that it is now suggested that matter/energy may have been everlasting; or alternatively it may have begun by a quantum variation in a vacuum (with gravitational and mass energy balancing so that the fluctuation had zero mass energy overall). But even if either of these were the case, we still have to ask why it is that energy has these characteristics? The simplest answer is that God gave them. I appreciate that none of these are knockdown arguments. It might be the case that matter and energy just exist and their characteristics are merely random and meaningless, but this is not the simplest explanation—in fact it is no explanation at all.

As we look at the development of the universe from

the Big Bang onwards, some 15 billion years ago, in fact we find an amazing set of coincidences, which have enabled evolution to take place in the universe as a whole, in the galaxies and the stars, and for life to evolve on Planet Earth and finally for intelligent life to emerge in the form of *Homo sapiens*.

I must not become too technical. And in any case to describe these 'coincidences' in detail would take a whole set of lectures, rather than a passing mention here. But I must give you some idea of what I am talking about. At first sight it may seem extraordinary that if the nature of things had been only slightly different from what it is, we would not be living in this universe in which we find ourselves. For example, there is a very delicate balance in the distribution of matter necessary to produce galaxies at all, with the consequent possibility of life on earth. The Big Bang occured in such a way as to make possible the eventual formation of galaxies with the consequent possibility of life on earth. The most ubiquitous objects in the universe are neutrinos; small, elusive, electrically neutral. If their weight were only just slightly more than it is, the strength of gravity in the universe as a whole would be increased, so that instead of its present expansion, the universe would actually be contracting. There is a kind of 'fine tuning' in the weight of a neutrino, so that galaxies and star clusters could readily form.

There are many other examples of fine tuning as we look at the universe. For example, if the mass of the universe were only slightly more than it is now, the force of gravity would have resulted in its collapse long before intelligent life could have formed. On the other hand, if matter were more abundant, the force of gravity would not have been as great and the expansion would have been greater, so that it has been calculated that stars and galaxies would not have been formed in their present abundance. Again, if the neutron mass were reduced to only .998 of its present value, there would be no hydrogen atoms at all—and our universe depends on the present balance of hydrogen and helium within it. And so I could go on, with coincidence after coincidence[4]. It is interesting, for example, that the process of burning hydrogen in the stars is so fine-tuned that carbon is produced, and then used up stars explode and planets such as ours are formed out of the debris. Our life processes on earth are carbon-based, so the fine-tuning is essential to life.

We may think it fortunate that water evolved, as this element also is necessary for life. It may seem strange that earth has evolved self-governing or cybernetic systems which have given stability to our environment, and thus ensured that circumstances were optimal for the evolution of life. For example, our present atmosphere evolved from a more primitive atmosphere, fortunately in such a way that life survived. There evolved a cybernetic system, involving living things, which ensures the stability of our present atmosphere. The proportion of gases is just right: a little more hydrogen, and lightning flashes would cause fires which could not be put out; a little less, and things would not burn at all. Again, there is a constant proportion of salt in the oceans, despite the fact that rivers carry down silt with large quantities of salt: a very slight difference only would mean that no cell could live in the oceans. Again, the heat of

4. I have set out these 'coincidences' in greater detail in *The Probability of God,* (SCM Press, 1985). I have borrowed the summary of my argument from a lecture by Dr. Joseph Needham given in Cambridge in December 1986.

the planet is maintained at a fairly constant average, despite the fact that over the aeons of time the luminosity of the sun has increased by some 30%.

As the number of 'coincidences' lengthens, and as their scope narrows from the universe to the planet, so it seems to me less and less probable that they should be purely random. It seems more and more probable that these 'coincidences' are intended (in accordance with the laws of nature), so as to make possible the emergence of man. This does not prove the existence of God, but it does, as I see it, make it very probable that these conditions are part of God's purpose for this world.

There is a sense in which all these 'coincidences' can be explained by the fact that we are here to observe them at this particular epoch in the development of the universe. Obviously they could not have taken place early in the history of the universe, because no star then would have been old enough to explode, and it is only through an exploding star that this planet has been able out of the debris to form with potentiality for life. The fact that we exist means that these 'coincidences' had to take place.

There is always the possibility that these 'coincidences' just happened, improbable as that might seem to us. But if there were an infinite number of universes, each with different natural constants, and each with different natural laws, then a universe like ours would be bound to occur. In that case, our universe could be a merely fortuitous occurrence. But it can be shown that it is extremely improbable that there is an infinite number of universes, all with different constants and laws from our own, about which we can know precisely nothing, since our own universe must be all that we can know—that, after all, is why we call it a 'universe'.

I mention these coincidences to show that, far from the natural sciences disproving God, they make it entirely reasonable to take the leap of faith which enables us to believe in him. If we are going to communicate the Gospel in a scientific age, people need to know about the way in which our modern knowledge of the evolution of the universe leads us towards God rather than in the opposite direction.

Scientists now look on matter very differently from the way in which they used to do. In the old days people thought of atoms as solid building blocks of matter. Nowadays they know that atoms are not solid at all. Harold Schilling has written:

As science has explored the micro-world within the atom it has not found anything to which the traditional notion of substance might be usefully applied[5].

When we get down to the smallest particles that are known to exist, matter it seems is fundamentally relational, ''much more like a delicate fabric of dynamic relationships than an edifice of hard building blocks''[6]. These elementary particles also have a tendency to be gregarious, to coalesce into larger and more complex structures; a tendency that they share with all living things within the evolutionary process.

The effect of such advances in knowledge is that the sciences are now wide open to a religious interpretation of life, and no longer tied to a totally materialist view. Furthermore, there is uncertainty apparently built into

5. H. K. Schilling, *The New Consciousness in Science and Religion*, (SCM Press, 1973), p. 25.
6. H. K. Schilling, *op. cit.*, p. 26.

the universe itself. It appears that at the micro-level, one can know either the speed of a particle or its location, but not both. It even seems—incredible as it may sound—that the observer actually influences the location of the particle which is under his observation.

Schilling contrasts the now out-dated 'modern' view of matter with the even more recent 'post-modern' view[7]:

> According to the former view the world was closed, essentially complete and unchanging, basically substantive, simple and shallow, and fundamentally unmysterious, a rigidly programmed machine. The second regards it increasingly as unbounded, uncompleted, and changing, still becoming, basically relational and complex, with great depth, unlimited qualitative variety, and truly mysterious—a restless, vibrant, living organism forever pregnant with possibilities for novel emergencies and developments in the future.

Clearly this 'post-modern' view of matter gives room for the Divine Creator working through his Holy Spirit within the universe which he has created, and makes it easier to see nature as declaring the glory of God. This way of thinking helps the communication of the Gospel in a scientific age.

The earlier view of nature regarded it as a machine, instead of a living organism. This viewpoint permeated science as a whole and was even applied to living organisms. The Oxford Professor, Sir Alister Hardy, contributed to the theory of evolution by pointing out that the initiatives of individual members of a species have helped the onward march of evolution within that

---

7. H. K. Schilling, *op. cit.*, p. 44.

species. He protested angrily against the mechanistic approach. He wrote[8]:

> I believe that the dogmatic assertions of the mechanistic biologists, put forward with such confidence as if they were the voice of true science when they are in reality the blind acceptance of an unproven hypothesis, are as damaging to the peace of mind of humanity as was the belief in miracles in the middle ages.

I have been trying in this lecture to think with you about how the Gospel appears in an age of science. Not long ago, the presumptions of scientific thinking helped to stop the ears of people to the communication of the Gospel, especially in an age in which science had made such tremendous leaps forward, and in which its application to the natural world in the form of technology had revolutionalised so many people's lives. I have tried to indicate that a more sympathetic outlook has recently emerged within the scientific world, as the scientists have penetrated more deeply into their subjects.

Yet it would be wrong to give the impression that there are no differences between the scientific and the religious outlooks. Part of the matter is that the two are looking in differing direction. As Professor A. N. Whitehead wrote more than half a century ago[9]:

> When you understand all about the sun and all about the atmosphere and all about the rotation of the earth, you may still miss the radiance of the sunset.

This is not entirely fair to scientists, who are very aware of beauty in their work, but it is a more

8. Alister Hardy, *The Divine Flame,* (Collins, 1966), p. 25.
9. A. N. Whitehead, *Science and the Modern World,* (Macmillan, New York, 1926), p. 286.

intellectual kind of beauty seen in the elegance of a scientific explanation rather than aesthetic beauty seen in the world of nature.

There is much truth in the view that there are differences in the levels of meaning to the questions asked by the sciences and religion. The sciences are looking for answers to 'How' questions, while religion is looking for an answer to 'Why' questions; although, as John Polkinghorne has pointed out[10], the two questions can at times seem to blur.

Perhaps the most obvious difference lies in the contrast between the scientific method and the way in which we approach religion. The sciences deal with objects that can be weighed and measured (although the micro-world of matter does not seem to be so solid and substantive as the macro-world in which we live). There are those who say that theology is also a science and works in a similar way[11], but this is not the case. Religion deals primarily with the transcendent God, and He by his very nature is not an object which can be weighed or measured. We can only experience the outskirts of his ways.

By contrast science examines the evidence, questions it and dissects it and then tries to explain the phenomena by means of a working hypothesis. But religious faith is not the same as a working hypothesis. Faith is God's gift to us, which enables us to respond in trust and confidence to him as he has disclosed himself in revelation. The sciences however proceed by doubt. For example, Newton discovered the laws of gravity by observing an apple fall to the ground. In fact these laws of gravity did not seem to be universally applicable:

10. J. Polkinghorne, *One World*, (S.P.C.K., 1986), p. 62.
11. Cf. A. Richardson, *Christian Apologetics*, (SCM Press, 1947), pp. 50ff.

for example they did not fit the orbit of Mercury, the planet nearest to the sun. Doubt arose as to whether they should be modified. Einstein was able to build upon them his hypothesis of general relativity which accounted for the discrepancies that had been noted.

Religion proceeds not by doubt, but by faith and acceptance. Yet the contrast is not absolute. For if Einstein had not had something akin to a flash of inspiration, he would not have formulated his laws of relativity; while the religious man not only has faith in God, but also may well question some aspects of God's revelation and, like Job, may voice his anger at complacent piety. It is perfectly proper for faith in God to coexist with healthy doubt about some of faith's intellectual formulae. Nonetheless, despite these similarities, there is a real contrast in outlook between science and faith. There is a sense in which the ultimate questions of science form the initial assumptions of religion.

This leads to a further difference between science and religion. Science wants to go on questioning and questioning, and to find a reason for everything in scientific terms. But when religion interposes with a 'personal' explanation which brings in God, then the scientific enterprise is at an end. There is no point in looking for scientific answers if God has interposed. And religious people have had a tendency to introduce God in the gaps of scientific knowledge, while scientists want to close those gaps with scientific knowledge. Religious people on the whole have not been overkeen to understand God as working through secondary causes.

Scientists certainly prefer simple solutions to scientific problems, partly because these are more elegant, but really because experience has shown them that the simplest solutions are most likely to be true. I suppose it could be said that to assert that God has interposed to do something is the simplest explanation of all. But it is simple *scientific* explanations that scientists prefer, rather than what they fear may be simplistic 'personal' explanations which involve God. It must be admitted that such 'personal' explanations have time and again been shown to be false. God does not send a thunderbolt; it is the result of particular metereological conditions. God does not send illness; it is the result of infection by a virus or by bacillae. God has not sent AIDS out of anger for immoral behaviour; the occurrence of AIDS can be given a perfectly adequate scientific explanation. We can only communicate the Gospel in a scientific age if we do not try to close the gaps. Scientists must be free to pursue scientific truth wherever it takes them without the Church making naive counterclaims for divine intervention.

The function of the sciences is to give an explanation of the natural world and the way in which its parts operate, in such a way that future events or movements can be predicted. Although the way in which the sciences function breeds certain attitudes of mind among scientists, the sciences themselves do not contain any particular world outlook. Indeed it is clear that scientists do differ in their beliefs, ideologies and outlooks. The task of integrating the different conclusions of the sciences into a coherent system belongs to a discipline called 'the philosophy of science', which is all too often confused with the sciences themselves. As Dr. P. E. Hodgson has written[12]:

12. In an as yet unpublished paper entitled ''Theology and Quantum Physics'' given at the Ian Ramsey Centre, Oxford University in the autumn of 1987.

You are free to base your physics on whatever philosophical presuppositions you choose, but this is a choice with momentous consequences. The inner logic of your choice will penetrate your physics, and it will flourish or decline in proportion to the truth of your chosen presuppositions. ''By their fruits you shall know them.''

I am aware that I have been speaking of the sciences as though I were referring only to the natural sciences. The human sciences of psychology, sociology and anthropology have flourished alongside the natural sciences, and they too have impeded the communication of the Gospel. Television programmes nowadays tend to include a psychologist rather than a priest, and sociologists and anthropologists are more in demand than theologians on such programmes. Why is this? It is partly because there is a feeling abroad that the human sciences give precision and professionalism where religion produces prejudice and amateurishness. Religion is felt to be out of date, old fashioned compared with the human sciences. The very word 'theology' has become in common parlance the equivalent of irrelevant theorising.

Psychology is the science of the working of the human psyche, its thinking and feeling and willing and deciding. Sociology is the science of group behaviour, the science of the development and nature and laws of human society. Anthropology is the scientific study of mankind, especially of its societies and customs, with special reference to the evolution of man as an animal. Although more recent writings in the human sciences have been more open to the truth that man has a human soul which enables him to be in relationship with God and to know his will, this viewpoint has barely filtered through to popular consciousness. As a result these sciences, as much as the natural sciences, tend to impede the communication of the Gospel in so far as they have contributed to the presumption that there is no God.

Freud is the name which occurs to most people when psychology is mentioned. Today Freud's work is often criticised because he took the malfunctioning of the psyche as the key to unlock its secrets. Nonetheless Freud has put us all in his debt by opening up the vast importance of the unconscious for the explanation of human attitudes, character and behaviour. His analysis of the psyche, with its ego, id and superego, is useful for the explanation it gives of how conscience developed. His views on religion are perhaps best described by the title of his book, *The Future of an Illusion*. His former colleague Jung by way of contrast saw religion as a fundamental human need, and found that the problems of the middle-aged were usually due to an interior spiritual vacuum. The fame and distinction of Jung has done something to mitigate the atheistic influence of Freud.

The differences between the many systems of psychology are so deep, and their methodologies seem so subjective, that it is hard to ascribe to it the status of a science. Psychology in itself has no direct bearing on the Gospel, for it only purports to explain how the psyche functions. It is the attitudes of mind that it engenders, and the presuppositions underlying its various systems that determine its ability to impede or to assist the communication of the Gospel.

The person who has exercised greatest influence in all parts of the world, so far as sociology is concerned, is Karl Marx. For him man was the result of social relations and economic forces.

Religion was the opiate of the masses because its consolations dulled their sense of injustice and so held back the revolution. Today there are those who combine a religious world view with an acceptance of the Marxist analysis of man, particularly in South and Central America. Nonetheless atheistic Marxism has stopped the ears of many from hearing the Gospel. We have already noted that in Russia so called 'scientific lectures' used to be given to eradicate the 'superstition' of religion; and perhaps it is because few today really believe full-blooded Marxist theory that there has recently been a thaw in that country towards the Church. There are of course many other sociologies than the Marxist one, and some of these help towards the communication of the Gospel. Strictly speaking sociology ought to be a science which explains social behaviour and the development of society, and (at least in the sociology of religion) it should assist our understanding of the development of religious bodies, but once again, it is the underlying presuppositions and the attitudes of mind that it engenders which influence the communication of the Gospel.

In anthropology it is the atheists again who have in the past often led the field. Konrad Lorenz concentrated on the aggressive instincts derived from man's animal past, while Desmond Morris, to use the title of his celebrated book, considers man to be nothing more than a 'naked ape'. Sociobiologists hold a reductionist view of human beings: E. O. Wilson begins his book on *Sociobiology* with the words:

The brain exists because it promotes the survival and multiplication of the genes that direct its assembly.

The human mind is a device for survival and reproduction, and reason is just one of its various techniques.

Man certainly has a body and an animal nature derived from his evolutionary past, and anthropology can be a useful science when it distinguishes this animal nature from what is distinctive of man made in the image of God. Once again, it is the underlying assumptions and attitudes that anthropology engenders which are important for the communication of the Gospel.

The human sciences, no less than the natural sciences, point beyond themselves to the God who has created human beings and made man in his own image. This is the intellectual high ground which is beginning to be reclaimed. But the sciences must speak for themselves. In so far as they are sciences, they must not be manipulated in favour of the Gospel any more than they should be used against the Gospel.

The Gospel of Jesus Christ is good news about God's great love for mankind, about his gracious action to renew us, to reclaim us and to rehabilitate us. It is a Gospel for everyone because it contains goods news for all. It is a Gospel about God, and this first lecture therefore has been concerned with the ways in which the sciences are often used to stop our ears from hearing God when in fact they should make it easier to communicate the gospel in a scientific age.

2

THE
GOSPEL AND THE SCIENCES

We are men and women of the late twentieth century. We can only hope to understand our faith as people of our time. We may try to put the clock back and pretend that we are living in a pre-scientific age, but we cannot hope to succeed. Even if we are successful in persuading ourselves, we shall not persuade other people.

The Gospels on the other hand were written in a pre-scientific age. Even more important, Jesus himself lived in a pre-scientific age. It is very difficult indeed for us to imagine the way people thought in those days. For example, we simply take for granted the law of cause and effect. We assume that every event has its preceding cause. But that was not so in Jesus's day. God was understood to be the direct cause of everything that happened. We too think of him as the cause of everything, but as the secondary cause, as working through events and people which together constitute the primary cause of all that happens. The ancient world had no idea of secondary causation. Of course people realised that some events in nature are regular—for example, night follows day in regular succession. This was not thought to be due to natural causes, as we understand them, but to the faithfulness of God.

Again, if today we want to know why unpleasant things are happening, we analyse just what is causing those undesirable events or happenings, so that we can stop them. Not so in the ancient world. If there was a drought, it was because God had shut up the heavens, probably because he was angry. If a person was ill, then some demon had got into him, and it was necessary to get rid of the demon. It was believed that God could give certain people miraculous powers so that they could impose their will on nature or on other people. Today we do not absolutely rule out that such powers may be possible, but we are extremely reluctant to admit that any miracle has taken place, and we prefer first to search for natural causes for some unusual event.

Even words in those days had a subtly different meaning. In any case the words of Jesus had to be translated from the original language in which they were spoken, that is, Aramaic, which bore the same kind of relationship to classical Hebrew as our English tongue today does to Anglo-Saxon. From Aramaic they were translated into Greek, which is the language of the New Testament, and from Greek into English. The meaning of English words also changes, as you can see by comparing the language of the Authorised Version with that of the New English Bible.

There are those who say that all these differences are such that it is not possible for us properly to appreciate what the people of New Testament times really meant.[1] A little reflection will, I am sure, convince you that this is not the case. While I do not want to minimise differences, it remains the case that the basic experiences of human beings are the same

1. D. E. Nineham, *The Use and Abuse of the Bible*, (Macmillan, 1976), p. 1.

down the centuries, and even if we have sometimes to re-interpret what they said and meant, we have little difficulty in appreciating that to which they were referring.

There is another great difference between their times and ours. We take for granted the idea of 'scientific history', that is to say, an ungarnished account of events and of what has caused them. And so when St. Luke wrote that 'as one who has gone over the whole course of these events in detail, he has decided to write a connected narrative' and when he calls this account 'authentic', we naturally tend to think that we are going to read 'scientific history'. But in those days 'scientific history' was unknown. People wrote for a purpose. Indeed all writing has a point and a purpose and it is necessary to consider its literary form in order to find out what the author meant by it. Only recently in English literature have people begun to ask questions about the structure of writing, and what it is that people are trying to convey.

Nowadays people are sometimes shocked to find out that, say, an Epistle which purported to be written by St. Peter can be shown by scientific literary criticism to have been not in fact written by him—they feel that this is a kind of deception. They have to learn that if someone in those days believed that he was writing with the authority of St. Peter behind him, it was an established literary convention for him to write as though the Epistle had actually been written by St. Peter.

Again, people are sometimes shocked when they are told that certain events which are recounted in the New Testament as though they were historical events did not actually happen. That is because in our day this would be regarded as quite misleading, rather like a journalist intentionally writing an incorrect report of an event that had not occurred. But if one looks at the literary form of the narrative, it may well be that the writer is trying to make a spiritual point through the story—what the Jews called a *midrash*—and he never intended it to be taken as literal truth. Or again, the writer may be using vivid poetic language in order to give the flavour of what he is trying to convey, and so he was not very concerned about giving an exact historical account.

It is well known that in the New Testament, of the four gospels one, St. John's Gospel, is very different from the other three. Although it contains probably some very early and authentic information, it was written by someone who looked back on events after they had passed. He understood Jesus very much in the light of his experiences of him as the Risen Lord, and his writing seemed to be almost like an inspired meditation. This gives us something of the literary form of the Gospel, for it is written in such a way that we are not always clear when we are reading the words of Jesus and when we are meant to understand them as the comments of the author.

In contrast to the Fourth Gospel, the other three gospels have an obviously close relationship with one another. For this reason they are sometimes known as the 'synoptic gospels'. Although these three gospels have an obvious similarity, closer inspection shows that they have many small but significant differences, and that these differences often form a pattern. They disclose the viewpoint of each author. We have to learn the truth that in the ancient world an author felt free to make these alterations in order to express his own viewpoint. We must not criticise this from our twentieth century point of view. The Gospels were written in the first century AD and they can only reflect the literary writing of that day. Scientific analysis of the New Testament along these literary lines helps us to get into the minds of the New Testament authors and to understand better the Gospel which they were proclaiming.

There are those who say that to use such techniques on the New Testament is to treat the Bible as if it were an ordinary secular work rather than the revealed Word of God. However, if the Bible really is the revealed Word of God, we need to be as rigorous as we can in the way in which we read it. Just because it is such an important book, we need to separate out the Word of God from the words of men. Nor should we think that all this necessarily takes us away from hearing God's word. Of course it can. We can be so concerned about minutiae and so preoccupied with sources, that we forget to allow its inspired message to sink into our hearts. We need to sit under the Bible to find the power, the promises and the presence of God. We need to concentrate on the essentials of the Gospel in the Scriptures, and we need to see a passage as a whole, and indeed the Bible as a whole. On the other hand, the scientific study of the Bible can have a wonderfully liberating effect. I shall always remember the excitement I felt when I first seriously studied the Bible in this way: it seemed to me that I could hear the Word of God where before I could not. I see that Dr. Runcie, the Archbishop of Canterbury, had a similar experience. He has written recently:

> The authority of scripture often seems to suffer as much from its adherents as from its detractors. Frequently its authority is thought to lie in some supposed inerrancy or infallibility that the church does

C

not claim for it, and to be impugned by the application of literary criticism. In fact I believe modern biblical study can be immensely stimulating, enriching the imagination, stirring the conscience and provoking new insights into the faith. We should rejoice in the wealth of variety of scripture, even admiring its intractability and resistance to the systematisers. Some people have said 'No one was ever converted by biblical criticism.' That's not true. I'm an example of it . . .'[2]

Before we look at particular instances where the sciences can help us today in our interpretation of the Gospel, let us first remind ourselves about the Gospel. The Scriptures are of course very important for our understanding of the Gospel, because they contain the earliest written records, and indeed the only reliable written records about Jesus, who is the centre and heart of the Gospel. The Gospel is the Good News that God has acted for all of us through the person of Jesus Christ. It is Good News because Jesus has shown us how to live, for he himself was a human person as we are. But he was also the Son of God and so his life conveys to us the Good News that God has accepted us as we are, even though we know that by our frailties and follies we are unacceptable to him. He has shown this by his sacrificial death on the Cross and, by raising Jesus from the dead, God has made clear his vindication of his Son and set his seal on the victory of the Cross.

Now if science could disprove the resurrection, that would indeed be a denial of the Gospel. Or again, if science could prove that Jesus was not crucified on the Cross, that would also deny the Gospel. Or if it could

2. R. A. K. Runcie, *Authority in Crisis?*, (SCM Press, 1988), pp. 35f.

be shown that Jesus was not a human being, or that he is not the Son of God, these also would deny the Gospel. Of course the sciences can do none of these things. So we need not approach the question about the impact of the sciences on the Gospel with any kind of fearfulness. On the contrary, we should look at the points where the sciences and the Gospel interact with eagerness and expectation. We may hope that they will shed some fresh light on our understanding of the Gospel and enable us to show real integrity in retaining our biblical faith and also remaining men and women of a scientific age.

The first point of interaction is the Creation. According to Genesis this took place in six days; and on the seventh day the Lord God rested. On the basis of genealogies in the Bible it was calculated by Bishop Usher that this event took place in 4004 BC. As there are two stories of Creation in the scriptures—Genesis chapters 1 and 2—it is not easy to combine the two. This in itself should give us an early warning that the biblical accounts are not intended to be 'scientific history', but rather poetic accounts of the relationship between God and his creation, using the current imagery of the time. (In one of these accounts the writer used the Babylonian creation story, but adapted it to show Jahwe, that is to say Almighty God, as the transcendent Creator.)

When we turn to the natural sciences, we find a very different account of creation. It is possible to calculate what happened to within a minute of the Beginning. Some 15 billion years ago there was an enormous explosion of which we can still measure the residual heat of some 3 degrees above absolute zero. What caused the explosion, no one really knows, although there is no lack of theorizing. Matter may have always been there; but it looks as though matter may have simply appeared in a vacuum. Quantum theory enables us to presume this, providing that the minute amount of matter/energy that appeared was paralleled by the negative energy of gravity, so that added together they came to zero energy. It has been calculated that there would have been a brief moment of enormously inflationary expansion. Then came the Big Bang, and in the first few moments after the Big Bang conditions for the rest of the evolutionary process were settled, with the right proportions of hydrogen and helium and the right rate of expansion; the right distribution of matter/energy and the right amount of heat to enable matter to form. Then came galaxies and then stars; and when certain stars had come to the end of their natural life, they exploded. Out of the debris new stars formed and occasionally out of the debris planets were formed too. In this kind of way Planet Earth came into being.

There then followed the whole wonderful story of evolution. First there appeared a very primitive form of life, probably in the oceans. These cells released oxygen, so that our atmosphere changed to its present form. A natural balance of nature enabled the salt content of the oceans to remain constant, despite inflows from rivers; and the average temperature also remained constant, despite an increase of some 30% in the luminosity of the sun. In these optimum conditions for the evolution of life, more and more complex forms emerged, first in the sea, and then on land and in the air. Small variations in the genetic structure of living beings naturally occurred, and those that were useful for survival or for reproduction naturally ensured the continuance of those individuals of a species which were endowed with such variations; and so evolution slowly but surely progressed.[3]

Finally man—*Homo sapiens*—emerged from this process a very short time ago, comparatively speaking. Man had certain unique properties of which we can find only vestiges elsewhere in the animal world. Man has the power to reflect on events, to handle abstract ideas, and to know the difference between right and wrong. He is therefore able to act as steward of all creation—if he is so minded—and also he is able consciously to enter into fellowship with God.

This picture of creation is radically different from the Six Days of Creation in Genesis chapter 1 and from the story of Eve being formed out of the rib of the first man Adam in Genesis chapter 2. The Genesis stories have great truths in them for which we rightly judge them to be inspired—the absolute sovereignty of God, his high valuation of creation—"behold it was very good"—its orderliness, and its hierarchical structure. The account in Genesis chapter 2 gives profound insights into relationships between man and the animals, relationships between the sexes, and the ambivalent nature of man, a mixture of good and bad. It was not intended to be a scientific account of nature, and I find myself rather embarrassed by the attempts of some Evangelical scientists to reconcile Genesis with what we can learn about origins from the natural sciences.[4]

As I see it, the scientific picture of origins which emerges from the natural sciences, although it is still tentative (because all scientific hypotheses are open to correction), nonetheless has about it a grandeur which

3. Cf my *Probability of God*, (SCM Press, 1985), pp. 23-58.
4. E.g., Alan Haywood, *Creation and Evolution*, (Triangle, 1985).

leads me to worship the Lord who created the process and the Holy Spirit who inspires the whole process. Creation, as scientists see it, has a far larger canvas both in time and in space, with an expanding universe, with thousands of millions of galaxies and literally billions and billions of stars. It gives us an insight into the depths of God's wisdom, and a vision of the greatness of the divine 'experiment', if we may so call it, which has called the worlds into being, and which has given such enormous responsibility to the human race with its unique characteristics. (There may be other intelligent beings elsewhere in the universe, but we do not know of them, and probably we never can.) Here, it seems to me, is an instance where science can enrich our vision of God in respect of his creation of the universe.

A second point of interaction concerns not the beginning but the end of the universe. There are some attempted descriptions of this in the Scriptures. In the Second Epistle General of St. Peter (3.10) we read, in explanation that the end of the world had not yet arrived:

> But the Day of the Lord will come; it will come, unexpected as a thief. On that day the heavens will disappear with a great rushing sound, the elements will disintegrate in flames, and the earth with all that is in it will be laid bare.

This sounds rather like a huge nuclear explosion, or the result of a vast meteorite crashing on earth. Of course either of these eventualities could happen. But I do not think that the author of this Epistle intended to make a scientific forecast of the future. I think that he was expressing in picture language some important truths, such as the suddenness and unexpectedness of

God's judgement on us, and that we ought therefore to strive at all times to be at peace with God, for we never know what is in store for us, or indeed how long we have on earth.

The Book of Revelation also contains visions of the end of the world. There are those who try to fit them in with actual happenings on earth, in the same way as the book of Daniel provides a happy hunting ground for such prophesies, for its passages are so vaguely worded that they can be taken to mean almost anything. In fact the literary form of this kind of literature is not really prophetic but apocalyptic, that is to say, a form of literature which used vivid poetic language about the future to underline the sovereignty of God and the urgent and pressing need for steadfastness and right behaviour here and now.

Another aspect of the Last Things in the New Testament is the belief in the Coming of Jesus at the end of time. In the early Church his Coming was thought to be imminent. We can see the viewpoint of someone like St. Paul changing over the years when the Second Advent did not take place. By the time of what is probably the latest Epistle in the New Testament—2 Peter, quoted above—the writer has to explain that 'a thousand years is like one day' (2 Peter 3.8). It is not of course impossible that Jesus Christ should return to earth, although the insight of St. John's Gospel that Jesus would return in the person of the Holy Spirit seems more profound. It is however more important that we should consider the truths that are intended by the use of this language, rather than commit ourselves to a literal belief in the Second Advent. These truths, as I understand them, are as follows: first, that we need always to behave as though the Last Judgement was upon us;

secondly, that God had a purpose in sending his Son into the world, and there will come a definite time when this purpose for the world will be complete.

Now if we contrast the scientific view of the end of the universe with that depicted in the scriptures, we find great differences. In the first place, the second law of thermodynamics, while it does not function within closed systems, holds good for the universe as a whole: heat is becoming more and more evenly distributed. The end of everything will be a heat death, when all energy is perfectly distributed throughout the universe. That will be the case if the universe continues to expand. However it is not clear that this expansion will continue for ever. The force of gravity pulls the universe in on itself, and the force of the initial explosion keeps on forcing it to expand. The universe is near the critical point where these two forces tend to be equal. If in time expansion ceases, the universe will implode back to the state of singularity in which it probably existed before the Big Bang. So far as the future of our planet is concerned, Professor Hoyle has described it as follows:

> The sun will grow steadily more luminous as its hydrogen supply is converted into helium, and this will go on until the oceans boil on the earth . . . as the sun grills the earth it will swell, at first slowly and then with increasing rapidity until it swallows the inner planets.[5]

Superficially there is a contrast between the biblical view of the End and scientific predictions. I do not see that this in any way detracts from the truth of the Gospel. I look to the sciences to predict the future,

5. F. Hoyle, *The Nature of the Universe*, (Blackwell, 1950), p. 86.

and I look to the Scriptures to give us inspired insights about our relationships with God and our fellow men.

I referred just now to the Second Advent of Christ. There are events connected with Christ's Advent in the first century BC which seem to be in conflict with scientific knowledge, particularly what is popularly known as the Virgin Birth, but which is more accurately described as the Virginal Conception. I do not intend now to argue the case for or against (that would involve weighing many considerations), but simply to show the differences, and how they can perhaps best be reconciled.

In the first place, no Christian could doubt that God, if he so wished, could have sent his Son into the world by means of a Virginal Conception. Even David Jenkins, the Bishop of Durham, has agreed to that, although I think his well publicised remarks against what he called a 'laser beam' miracle were particularly unfortunate.[6] He caused great offence by suggesting that people who did believe in the Virgin Birth were fools, and by accusing God of monstrous behaviour if he worked a miracle in the conception of his Son, but did not do so when the Jews were being exterminated in the Holocaust by the Nazis. He did not seem to realise that many who do believe in the Virginal Conception are not fools, or that by his own moral criterion all right desires put into our hearts by God are equally open to his objection about 'laser beam miracles'.

What are the scientific facts about the Virginal Conception? There are many examples of parthenogenesis in nature: aphids for example reproduce

6. Cf. D. Jenkins, *God, Miracle and the Church of England*, (SCM Press, 1988), p. 5.

without male participation. Some species combine both parthenogenesis and sexual intercourse as means of reproduction. With the species of *Homo sapiens*, however, the only means of reproduction is through the fertilisation of an ovum by male sperm. Both the man and the woman contribute equally to the genetic make up of a new human being. One may properly ask: if Jesus did not have any human male chromosomes, how did he get the right number of chromosomes that every human being has to have? We can hardly believe that he had a double number from his mother, for that would be very difficult to account for in one ovum. If on the other hand his 'female' chromosomes were miraculously created, they would still have to be particular chromosomes bearing particular characteristics. What were these? We cannot say that they were God's, because God does not have chromosomes; and in any case the doctrine of the Incarnation is not about a half-man, half-God: it concerns God becoming man, with a full and complete human nature, just as Christ's divine nature was full and complete.

It follows from this that, while scientific knowledge can never rule out the possibility of miracle, it is hard for us to understand what advantage would be gained by effecting the Incarnation by means of a Virginal Conception, while there do seem disadvantages, as I have indicated above.

In the light of these scientific facts, it seems sensible to look again at the reasons underlying the stories of the Virginal Conception in the only two passages in the New Testament where it is mentioned. In St. Matthew's Gospel a proof text is used—'A virgin shall conceive and bear a son'—which did not originally apply to Mary, and which did not even refer to a virgin in the original Hebrew. This suggests that belief in the Virginal Conception was already current when St. Matthew's Gospel was written, and the author was looking for some means to validate it. The author of the Gospel understands the belief to imply that 'God is with us'—in other words, that the infant Jesus is the Son of God. For the same reason he writes that Mary 'found she was with child by the Holy Spirit'. The story is important because it shows a conviction that the Incarnation really took place right from the first beginnings of the life of Jesus. When we turn to St. Luke, we find not a dream, but the appearance of an angel; both, incidentally, symbols of divine revelation. Although the story here is very different, and told in more poetic imagery, the point is the same: to show that Jesus is 'the Son of the Most High' and is a true successor to David, from whom the Messiah was expected.

We have to realise that, in those days, the facts about human reproduction were unknown. The woman was thought to be a kind of funnel or container in which the male seed grew into a human being. The only way in which one could show that in Christ God had made a new start, that he had indeed sent his Son to be born as a human being, was through a story such as that of the Virginal Conception. It seems therefore that the truths for which the story of the 'Virgin Birth' stands can be (and indeed are) deeply held by many Christians without their believing in the historical event of a virginal conception.

However, science can never disprove the possibility of a miracle: and there are many Christians who do believe in the 'Virgin Birth' of Jesus. It is found in the Creed, which summarises the beliefs of Christians down the centuries.

As a result of the controversy stirred up by the Bishop of Durham, the bishops of the Church of England issued in 1986 a statement on the Nature of Christian Belief. We said:

As regards the Virginal Conception of our Lord we acknowledge and uphold this belief as expressing the faith of the Church of England, and as affirming that God has taken the initiative for our salvation by uniting with himself our human nature, so bringing to birth a new humanity.[7]

But we also added: "There must always be a place in the life of the Church for both tradition and enquiry."[8]

This Statement also considered the miracle of the Resurrection of Jesus. Here the situation seems rather different from that of the Virginal Conception. In the latter case there is some New Testament evidence of a tradition other than that of the Virginal Conception. But there is no tradition in the New Testament which suggests that Jesus's resurrection did not take place; and indeed it would be very difficult to account for the existence of the Christian Church without such a belief. The resurrection of Jesus was not in doubt in the New Testament, nor is it generally in doubt within the Christian Church. The doubt to which the Bishop of Durham drew attention concerns not the resurrection, but the mode by which it took place; whether it was a physical resurrection, or purely spiritual, and whether the tomb in which Jesus was buried bears witness to the fact that there was indeed a physical

7. *The Nature of Christian Belief*, (Church Ho. Publishing, 1986), p. 2.
8. Ibid.

resurrection.

I myself find it difficult to account for the story of the Empty Tomb unless Jesus was raised from the dead, so that the tomb was empty. I cannot take seriously the idea that Jesus recovered in the Tomb, somehow removed the stone from the inside, and then escaped. In the first place he was certified as dead, secondly no man would have had the strength for such a feat after crucifixion, and thirdly where did he go? Nor can I take seriously the idea that his disciples stole the body. Jews would not touch a dead body (except in preparation for burial), and in any case there was no martyr cult that grew up around his tomb. Nor would the Roman soldiers have stolen the body or they would have produced it. The idea that the women went to the wrong tomb and found it empty is a counsel of despair. Common criminals were usually put into the common grave, but the Gospel makes it clear than an exception (for which there are precedents) was made in his case. My own conclusion is that the tomb was empty because God raised Jesus from the dead. But it was not a resuscitation. The resurrection appearances were not those of an ordinary living person nor is there any suspicion of a 'second death' of Jesus later. It was a resurrection to a new mode of existence.

Such a resurrection seems to be unique (Bishop John Robinson tells a story of a Buddhist saint, but this does not provide a real parallel).[9] The natural sciences are not concerned with unique events. They always strive to find explanations within the natural regularities of existence. It is possible that the physical resurrection of Jesus is in accordance with some unknown spirit-

9. J. A. T. Robinson, *The Human Face of God,* (SCM Press, 1973), p. 139n.

ual law which supersedes the usual laws of physical nature; but if so, we know nothing about such a law. The biological sciences have a particular problem here in that the brain, when deprived of oxygen by physical death, quickly deteriorates, and cannot function properly after a short period. It seems likely that at this key point there is a real clash between the Christian faith and explanations that can be given by the natural sciences. But that, I believe, should not worry us. All laws, both spiritual and physical, come from God the Creator. At this key point of his self-revelation, when he wished to validate the saving death of his Son, and to show his vindication of Jesus, it seems entirely appropriate that he should, if he so desired, have abrogated his own laws in order to show that the ignoble death of Christ was indeed the means by which he reconciled the world to himself.

I have spoken about the physical Resurrection, as the greatest miracle of our Christian faith. There are of course many other miracles to be found in the Bible. They tend to 'cluster' round four periods[10]: those of Abraham, Moses, Elijah and Elisha, and the ministry of Jesus. Legends tended to grow up around great men, and especially religious leaders, and it is not too difficult, if we so wish, to find a naturalistic explanation for many if not all of the miracles of the Old Testament.

When we turn to the New Testament, however, the position is different. There can be little doubt that Jesus did do remarkable things, as otherwise he could not have been so well known throughout Judaea and Galilee

10. D. L. Edwards *Essentials,* (SCM Press, 1988), p. 177 has only three such clusters; but it is surely necessary to include the miraculous birth of children to Abraham in extreme old age, from which began the drama of divine redemption.

in the three short years of his public ministry. His mighty works may be divided into healing miracles, including resuscitations, and nature miracles. I do not think that we need have any real difficulties about the healing miracles from the point of view of the natural sciences. It is now beginning to be more widely realised that there are psychosomatic factors in health and healing, and that the personality of a healer has a large part to play in the healing of a sick person.

In the ancient world the physical laws governing health and healing were largely unknown, and when Jesus was believed to cast out demons, in fact he had, through his spiritual influence and power, enabled a person to speed up his natural healing processes, so that cures (physical, mental and spiritual) were, as it were, instantaneous. Comparisons between the synoptic gospels show the ease with which, in those days, stories could be altered and embellished in their details, and this may account for some factors in the healing stories, especially concerning dead persons. Since in those days it was not possible to be certain about the moment of death, it could be that resuscitations were really revivals of consciousness.

The nature miracles seem in a different category. It might be that there are naturalistic explanations of some miracles, such as the feeding of the five thousand. Again, we have to look at what these stories are telling us rather than their historical veracity, which is a twentieth century rather than a first century pre-occupation. For example, Peter's walking on the water, and subsequent sinking, tells a story of faltering faith. The calming of the tempest tells the story of Jesus's ability to calm anxious and fearful hearts. Once again, there is no doubt that God can work miracles if he is so minded, since he is the author and creator of all things. The question we must ask is whether it seems consonant with God's purpose that he should have frequently intervened in this way throughout the ministry of Jesus. There are those who believe that he did, and they are fully entitled to this conviction. Those who live in a scientific age may prefer a naturalistic explanation of many of these stories, but they cannot deny the claim of miracle: the most they can do is to say that miracles must be very exceptional and naturalistic explanations should be sought, since many events which in the past were regarded as miraculous have been given a perfectly natural explanation through advances in scientific knowledge.

The subject of this course of lecutures is *Communicating the Gospel in a Scientific Age* and I have been attempting to show what kind of light the natural sciences can shed on the Gospel itself. I must turn for a moment to the human sciences.

Sociology is the science of the customs, traditions and laws of society and a study of its development. It is one area in which considerable advances are being made in New Testament scholarship. It is helpful to understand the social background of the province of Judaea and the tetrarchy of Galilee in the time of Jesus, and to read for example his teaching on marriage and the family in the light of the social customs of his day. Without this background knowledge it is not easy to answer the question: "If Jesus in his society taught what he did, what does his teaching mean for us in our twentieth century society in Britain today?"

Again if we study the economics of first century Palestine, we can understand more of the appeal of Jesus to the landless labourers in a country with many absentee landlords. We can realise some of the reasons why the priestly hierarchy, with its vested interests, tended to be opposed to him. We can also apply psychological insights to the Gospel. When the madman who was cutting himself in the tombs was asked his name by Jesus, he replied: "Legion". A psychological explanation of this could be that he had suffered violence at the hands of a Roman legion in the past, and this accounted for his pathological condition. On the other hand it could be that he was suffering from a dissociated personality, and his reply indicated that he did not really feel conscious of a personal identity, a condition which Jesus healed. The difficulty with all such explanations is that they appear to be subjective and uncertain, yet psychology certainly can shed some light on the Gospel.

I have tried in this lecture to show how the sciences, and mainly the natural sciences, when these are brought to bear on the Christian Gospel, can help us to understand it better. We are people of our time. We cannot pretend that we do not live in a scientific age. We need to interpret the Gospel in such a way that we remain loyal to its message and yet understand it in terms which enable us to retain our integrity as people of our age.

I believe that we can do this.

3

COMMUNICATING THE GOSPEL IN A SCIENTIFIC AGE

There was really no need to invite a Sassenach to come north of the Border to talk to you about *Communicating the Gospel in a Scientific Age.* I say this because I found among my books a much neglected volume of the Warrack Lectures for 1953. Called *Preaching in a Scientific Age*, it was written by that great Scottish divine, Archie Craig, who was at one time actually living and working in Glasgow as a Lecturer in Biblical Studies. I have not mentioned this in the earlier lectures, for fear that, if you knew, you would prefer to get his book out of the library rather than attend any more of my lectures! Dr. Craig's lectures were delivered thirty five years ago, but they still retain their freshness; and although at that time he took up perhaps a more traditional viewpoint about the historicity of most biblical miracles than I might wish to do, I think that in many ways our approach is similar.

Dr. Craig was concerned with preaching, which is a particular form of Gospel communication. This is not an activity, I hasten to add, that I wish in any way to undervalue, especially as I come from a church tradition with a poor preaching reputation, to speak in the Kirk which is renowned for its pulpit oratory.

Because Dr. Craig was preoccupied solely with preaching, he expressed himself with some force about the need to communicate the whole biblical message rather than to attempt to introduce a congregation to the niceties of biblical criticism. When people were hungering after spiritual bread, he warned against offering merely critical stones, "doling out J, E and P (the sources of the Pentateuch) as though they were the very latest thing in evangelical vitamins"[1]; and he told his audience "to accustom your people to study the Bible with a telescope as well as under a microscope"[2].

What I find particularly interesting about the background of Dr. Craig's lectures is that the credibility of science was much higher in his day than it is today. He quoted at length from a contemporary book by Mr. W. A. Whitehouse[3], and I would like to repeat that quotation thirty five years later:

> Scientific thinking (wrote Mr. Whitehouse), bearing fruit in an all-pervading scientific attitude, promises to supply the resources by which man's economic standard of living may be raised, and all his capacities for good living can be developed. It is possible, according to this scientific faith, to organize life in a rational way so as to eradicate the international frictions leading to war and economic conflict. It is possible to produce and distribute man's wordly goods fairly and sensibly. For the first time in history man will have the opportunity and incentive to break free from the petty squabbles and sordid "necessities" which act today as a powerful break on his develop-

1.   A. C. Craig, *Preaching in a Scientific Age,* (SCM Press, 1948), p. 48.
2.   A. C. Craig, *op. cit.,* ibid.
3.   W. A. Whitehouse, *Christian Faith and the Scientific Attitude.*

ment. Provided man can be cured of his stupidity, human nature, like the world itself, will slowly reach perfection here in history. And the cure for stupidity is education in the scientific attitude.[4]

I think that a generation and a half later we have become more disillusioned with the ability of the sciences to alleviate the human situation. In the first place, we know something now of the dangers of technological innovation based on new scientific knowledge, whether these be fluorocarbons for our refrigerators and aerosols, or lead to increase the volatility of our petrol, or nuclear energy to keep our houses warm in winter. People may think that science has disproved the existence of God, but nonetheless they are somewhat disillusioned with the effects of science on their lives. Secondly we see that, despite all that the sciences can contribute, the world is still in a mess, with tension between East and West, gross inequality between North and South, and petty squabbles continuing unabated.

Dr. Craig gives a further quotation from Mr. Whitehouse which I should like also to reproduce because of the contrast it affords between then and now:

The common man is inevitably inspired to try and think scientifically about his personal affairs, and, more and more, he pins his hopes of happiness and success on ''doing things scientifically'' . . . When he is tangled up in personal and emotional difficulties, he knows perfectly well that a parson will say things to him that will only leave him battling with the same temptations after twenty years, so he turns to the psychiatrist for a ''scientific cure''. His very superstitions can be drawn into pseudo-scientific channels, as the more entertaining advertisements prove.

4.   W. A. Whitehouse, *op. cit.*, p. 28.

Anything that purports to be a scientific prescription for radiant living commands his attention, even if he does retain enough sense to keep his money in his pocket. I am qualified to speak a little scornfully (Mr. Whitehouse concluded), for in describing him I describe myself.[5]

Thirty five years later people may frequently watch psychologists and psychiatrists on television, but they do not consult them in vast numbers, and it is a long time since I saw an advertisement for a 'scientific preparation'.

I think therefore that we are in a somewhat healthier situation than we were then, in as much as we no longer adulate the sciences.

How do we communicate with people in a scientific age? Dr. Craig concentrated on preaching, and I do not propose to do that in this lecture, for two reasons. For an Anglican to come to Scotland to give hints on pulpit communication would be the ecclesiastical equivalent of carrying coals to Newcastle. But there is a second reason in addition to such personal modesty. Thirty five years ago churchgoing was still a conventional activity, so that it was possible to communicate from the pulpit with occasional churchgoers and with people who are perhaps best described as benevolent agnostics. But the position is different today, except for such special occasions as weddings and funerals (and perhaps also baptisms, but to a diminishing extent). The preacher communicates today from the pulpit only with the charmed circle of his regular congregation. Other forms of communication are necessary if the Gospel is to reach the vast unchurched masses of the population.

5.   W. A. Whitehouse, *op. cit.*, p.30.

There is only one period in life when a person today in this land must receive religious education, and that is during his or her schooldays. I fear that we have neglected or underestimated the importance of Religious Education in schools, despite the fact that, until the new Education Act introduces a core curriculum, R.E. is the only complusory subject in the syllabus. Alas, this subject is often badly taught. This is partly, God help us, because there are not sufficient teachers prepared to teach it; it is partly because we have become so obsessed with religious pluralism that some teachers seem afraid even to name the name of Christ. They prefer to confuse the minds of young people with a mishmash of comparative religion. Worst of all, many headteachers, although this is against the law, only provide for R.E. in the lower grades of a comprehensive school. And so at the very time when young minds should be stretched to look for the religious message of the scriptures in the light of scientific criticism of the Bible and when they should be encouraged to measure the claims of the Gospel against the popular presuppositions of our predominantly materialist culture, the impression is given in our schools that religion is only for juniors. And so, as children grow up, they naturally graduate to the agnostic attitudes which spring from secular humanism.

So our best means of communicating the Gospel is removed from us—not that it should be used to indoctrinate the young but rather to put before them what is involved in being a Christian. There is a real hope that, as a result of the new Education Act, this disastrous situation will be to some extent remedied—if there are sufficient teachers for the subject.

A further means of communicating the Gospel in this

age of mass communications is to make better use of the communications media themselves. The Greek word for preaching is *kerussein,* to act as a town cryer, which (apart from propaganda on coins) was the only means of mass communication possible in the ancient world. Today we have others. Television sets are no longer a luxury but a necessity of life, so most people in this country think, and many would prefer to deprive themselves of food rather than of TV. But according to the laws of the land the Church is in some difficulty here. Advertisements for a particular church or religion are not permitted. Arrangements for television programmes are not in the hands of the churches but of the BBC or the television companies concerned. Furthermore, television is not a good teaching medium. Watching TV is rather like listening in to a conversation. What comes over best in this medium is not religious education, but a religious attitude of mind, religious commitment and authenticity, and these are often best conveyed by a passing remark and spontaneous response rather than by a specifically religious programme.

The situation in the USA is very different from here, and supplies us with a salutary warning. There the 'televangelists' may buy programme time. This however is very expensive, and so vast amounts of money have to be raised in order to purchase this television time. The programme itself constitutes the only opportunity for raising this money. It therefore tends to become a 'hard sell', and , as we have seen lately, those who deal in these vast sums are open to the temptations they bring. We may therefore be thankful for our British arrangements for religious television, although, with the impending advent of satellite television, and with 'dish aerials' costing under £200, the position is likely soon to alter for the worse after the American model.

There are of course other mass media, in particular the daily and weekly papers and magazines. Again, these are in private hands. Many national papers are now quite secularised and often those who write letters in their correspondence columns are not the people best calculated to communicate the Gospel.

Without doubt the best means of communicating the Gospel is from person to person, and in particular from lay person to lay person. The laity after all comprise 99% of the church. They are in touch with people in all strata of society. In the past there has been a tendency, at least in the Church of England, to leave the communication of the Gospel to the minister. But his time is limited and so are the number of people whom he can meet and with whom he can speak on such matters. In any case he is popularly thought to be 'paid to say that sort of thing'. When a lay man or woman declares his or her heart to another lay person, and shows how much the Gospel means to his or her life, this can have an immense effect. This is communication by life and character as much as by words. Such a person can speak in private conversation modestly, quietly and perhaps even haltingly about his faith; but his integrity and commitment nevertheless shine through what he says.

Many lay people feel unequipped to speak about the Gospel even in private conversation. They feel ignorant about the Christian faith, and vulnerable to difficult questions. I think that there is now appearing a thirst for better knowledge about and understanding of the Christian faith among lay people. I was always surprised at the numbers of lay people who came forward to

Foundation Courses, when we began these in the Diocese of Birmingham. I am sure that here is an activity which the Church needs to develop. In the Church of England we found it necessary to run these courses at diocesan level, and I think that the Church of Scotland, if it is not doing so already, should attempt them at least at presbytery level.

Here I speak in a general way about communicating the Gospel, but we must remember that, while we live in a scientific age, people are still people, whatever kind of age they live in. Even scientists have normal childhoods, normal marriages and normal children, and like the rest of us they have to face the inevitability of death. Science is an abstract subject—it is removed from the world in so much as it is an attempt to understand aspects of the world by standing back from them, abstracting a small part of them, and attempting to analyse their constituents, and to find the principles on which these exist and operate.

But scientists are different. They are human beings. They engage in scientific activity, to be sure, but only for a portion of their waking hours. It is a rare person to whom what is abstract means more than what is personal. We have only to observe how newspapers personalise the news to realise where people's interests really lie. And so, even in a scientific age, the communication of the Gospel best takes place in a personal setting and in connection with personal situations. It is specially relevant to feelings of fear, guilt, loss, failure, frustration and meaninglessness, as well as to the positive emotions of love, confidence, joy and success in personal relationships. Human relationships point in many ways to our relationship with God. For example, marriage is a fairly universal state of life in a scientific age as in any other, and there are many aspects of love and marriage which mirror the Gospel, and provide an analogy of our relationship to God.

We are, however, handicapped in communicating the Gospel by the culture in which we live, which is derived not only from the traditions of Christendom, but also from the Enlightment and from scientific pre-suppositions. For example, it is part of our culture that we make a fairly sharp division between facts and values. Facts, it is presumed, lie in the public domain: they can be shown to be either true or false. But values, it is assumed, constitute private options in a pluralist society which an individual may or may not wish to adopt.[6]

This polarisation arises from false thinking and has unfortunate results. In the first place, facts always carry with them a certain degree of interpretation, and this interpretation may be disputed. For example, if we consider the smallest particle of matter, say, the gluon, this can never be observed, and its existence is due to a particular interpretation of particle physics, about which not all may be agreed. Secondly, facts are never certain and seldom complete. They are always subject to modification, as when Newton's law of gravity was refined by Einstein's relativity theorems. Facts are falsifiable, and although there may be a very high degree of presumption that a certain fact is right, absolute certainty is not available.

As for values, if these are simply regarded as options for individual choice, modern society must lack any agreed body of values, and so lose its coherence, and

6.   Cf. L. Newbigin, *Foolishness to the Greeks*, (SPCK, 1986), pp. 16ff.

may even be threatened with collapse. While we may grant that it is not always easy to find all our values from the natural law, yet experience shows that some values are true, such as the unique value of each human being; and some are false, such as a viewpoint which places personal aggrandisement above the common good. In any case Christians believe that values have been divinely disclosed by God's self-revelation in Jesus Christ. Once the modern mind has grasped the falsity of this polarity between facts and values, it is open to accept the abiding truth of Christian values, and a person is open to commitment to Christ and his Gospel.

It is not a mere coincidence that in this scientific age in which we live, the Holy Shroud of Turin has excited much interest, with its negative image of a figure thought to be that of the crucified Jesus. I must admit to a great interest over many years for this 'relic', and indeed I chaired the 1977 London Conference on the Shroud. For me the attraction has been the deployment of scientific techniques in connection with something mentioned in the Gospels and closely connected with central events of the Christian faith.

In the popular mind however the interest has been rather different, as though the authentication of the Shroud through scientific techniques could in some way authenticate the Gospel itself. There are some who have suggested that the image on the Shroud consists of scorch marks caused by the moment of resurrection itself![7] Indeed I have even heard it said that it is through the providence of God that the Shroud has come to the fore in this sceptical and scientific age which,

---

7.   Cf. J. A. T. Robinson, 'The Shroud and the New Testament' in *Twelve More New Testament Studies,* (SCM Press, 1984), p. 91f.

like St. Thomas of old, requires material proof of the Resurrection (John 20.25).

As I prepare these lectures the carbon dating test is actually being carried out on a piece of linen from the Shroud, and it will soon be known whether this scientific technique attests that the linen belongs to the first century, or to a later period, in which case the image would be a fake. However even if the linen were shown to belong to the first century, this would not prove that it had been wrapped around the dead body of Jesus, or that the negative image imprinted on it is that of *his* dead body. There is now some evidence that negative imaging on a piece of cloth is not unique[8], and this suggests that the image on the Shroud does not consist of scorch marks. In any case scorch marks could not prove the transhistorical character of the Resurrection when Jesus passed into a different mode of glorified existence.

It follows therefore that the Shroud could never authenticate faith in the Risen Lord. The most that could be deduced from evidence that the Shroud does belong to the first century AD is that it provides some material corroboration of an object attested in the Gospels (which no one with any knowledge of Jewish burial customs of the time could ever have doubted existed). It would strongly suggest that Jesus was buried in a tomb (from which the Shroud was salvaged) as recorded in the Gospels, rather than in the common grave which was usually the resting place of criminals, as some hostile critics have suggested. It would also tell us

8.   Cf. *British Society for the Turin Shroud Newsletter*, 19, April 1988, p.5f, for details of a 39 year old West Indian who died in a Liverpool hostel and left his negative image on the mattress, and a not dissimilar occurrence at the Paracelsus Klinik, Silbersee, W. Germany.

something about the physical appearance of Jesus, a matter which may evince great interest today, but in which the Evangelists seem to have been profoundly uninterested. In these ways (and in these ways only) the Shroud could be an aid to faith. Even if the Shroud were thought to be authentic, it would always remain secondary to faith. Christianity is not about confidence in the authenticity of an object: it is about faith in God who raised his Son from the dead, and made him to sit in the heavenly places. This faith does not come from the sciences: It is a gift from God.

I have been speaking of Jesus being raised from the dead, and the use of the word 'raise' suggests an upward movement. The same is the case when we speak of the ascension of Christ. We commonly think of a three decker universe, with heaven above our heads, and hell beneath our feet. Professor Rudolf Bultmann, for many years the doyen of New Testament scholarship, found, during his war service as a chaplain in the 1939-45 war, that the soldiers under his pastoral care could make nothing of this, as it was so foreign to the way in which they thought as men of the twentieth century.

Bultmann therefore proposed that the Gospel should be demythologised, that is to say, removed from the cultural setting in which the Gospel took shape. Bultmann believed that if this were done, it would become credible again to modern man. He wrote

There is nothing specifically Christian about the mythical view of the world as such. It is simply the cosmology of a pre-scientific age.[9]

9.   R. Bultmann, 'New Testament and Myth' in *Kerygma and Myth*, (ed. H. W. Bartsch) (SPCK, 1962), p.3.

What Bultmann did was to discard such views and to preach the Gospel in such a way that it became an existentialist experience which required no knowledge about the historical Jesus save that he existed. Salvation became an existential response to the Word of God preached by words of men. This resulted in a Gospel which was so bare, so historically sceptical and so removed from worldly existence, that Bultmann seemed to have thrown out the baby with the bathwater.

Nonetheless Bultmann had pointed to a crucial issue. The Gospel as it was encapsulated in first century imagery is no longer credible to twentieth century man living in a scientific age. What is required is not demythologisation, but remythologisation. But this must be done in such a way that it retains the essentials of the Gospel while discarding the first century wrappings and substituting contemporary packaging. To what extent are the wrappings part of the Gospel itself? Is the Gospel capable of being translated into different imagery without destroying its essential nature? Focussed on those questions there has been in this country, if not much light, certainly a great deal of heat.

I refer to the publication twenty five years ago of Bishop John Robinson's *Honest to God*. Why was it that this rather confused little book sold over a million copies, and was translated into many languages? It was partly because of a headline in the Observer newspaper *"Our image of God must go"*, which gave a rather misleading impression of the book, because Bishop Robinson was not, as popularly thought, trying to destroy the traditional concept of God, nor did he seek to disturb those believers who were content with their traditional faith.

Bishop Robinson was a personal friend of mine, and

I think he is a very misunderstood person. He was passionate in his desire to communicate the Gospel to the masses of people to whom, in this scientific age, it was no longer credible. He borrowed from the ideas of Paul Tillich and suggested a fundamental change of imagery about God. He wrote[10]:

> The break with traditional thinking to which I believe we are now summoned is considerably more radical than that which enabled Christian theology to detach itself from a literal belief in a localised heaven. The translation from the God 'up there' to the God 'out there' though of liberating psychological significance, represented no more than a change in spatial symbolism.

Bishop Robinson was looking for a more drastic change. His eyes were first opened to the transformation that seemed to come over much of the traditional religious symbolism when it was transposed from the heights to the depths when he read a sermon of Paul Tillich published in his collection *The Shaking of the Foundations*. Why did this symbolism so appeal to him? I suspect for two reasons. In the first place, it is not uncommon to experience God deep within ourselves, as though the greater our self-knowledge becomes, and the more we penetrate into the ground of our being, the nearer we feel to God. And then secondly, as we learn more of the way in which evolution in this universe has developed, it is more and more clear that it is not God 'out there' who has been directing the process and interfering with nature, but rather God the Holy Spirit who has been working from within it, helping and enabling a development which reaches its

10.   J. A. T. Robinson, *Honest to God*, (SCM Press, 1963), p.21f.

culmination in intelligent life which is able consciously to worship God.

From the correspondence which Bishop Robinson received, it is clear that many people felt liberated by this simple reversal of religious symbolism.[11] At the same time I do not think that we can say that to substitute depth for height in out thinking about God is a theological improvement, unless we are prepared to identify the universe with God. If we believe that God is transcendent, there must be a sense in which he is beyond the bounds of the universe. Of course he is not located in space at all, nor is he bounded by it. To use the biblical phrase, 'in him we live and move and have our being' (Acts 17.28). The fact that we have to use the word 'transcendent' in this connection is significant, because even that word comes from a Latin root which means 'to overstep' or 'to surmount'. Moreover, this notion of transcendence accords with our actual experience of God, such as it is; for he comes to us as the One who is the 'beyond in our midst'.

It is a pity that, after the 'Honest to God' furore, the remythologisation debate has languished. It briefly surfaced in a further furore over the Birmingham symposium *The Myth of God Incarnate*[12]; but that concerned the doctrine of Christ rather than the doctrine of God, and the collection of essays was too thin and incoherent to begin a serious debate.

It is important, in communicating the Gospel to this scientific age, that we do use symbolism which is alive and meaningful today. This holds good generally, and not merely in connection with scientific symbolism,

11. Cf. D. L. Edwards, *The Honest to God Debate,* (SCM Press, 1963), pp. 84ff.

12. *The Myth of God Incarnate* ed. J. Hick (SCM Press, 1977), p. 12.

which has only a limited utility, because in religion we need symbols that are personal rather than abstractions from reality. Symbols may become outdated. Comparatively few people (south of the border, at any rate) have had much experience of a shepherd, and certainly not of the kind of shepherd who cared for sheep and goats in the ancient world, rough men who led their flocks rather than followed them from behind. Again, the symbol of a king when used for God has only a limited usefulness in a country which for some centuries has grown accustomed to a constitutional monarchy.

Some symbols, however, seem to endure for ever, especially if they derive from what Karl Jung called the archetypes of mankind's collective unconscious. There are other symbols which derive from the sciences, whether the human or the natural sciences, which have a real if limited usefulness.

Let me exemplify this by reference to the doctrine of justification by faith. This has held an important place in all reformed theologies, and in the case of Martin Luther it was central. Perhaps because of its very centrality, it has been a cause of controversy in the past between Catholics and Protestants, now happily settled. Mankind, because of universal sinfulness, is unrighteous. But through the righteousness of God, and by the sacrificial death of Christ, we are 'justified' or put in the right with God, and it is through faith that we grasp this great gift of forgiveness and rejoice in the restoration of our right relationship with him.

St Paul used the imagery of the law court in his portrayal of this great doctrine, but in these days such imagery has lost much of its appeal, and indeed it was never wholly apt, for God is best imaged not so much as a just judge as a loving father. Paul Tillich used the psychological image of 'acceptance' in order to illuminate this central truth for the twentieth century. In *Courage To Be* he wrote:

> In the centre of the Protestant courage of confidence stands the courage to accept acceptance in spite of consciousness of guilt . . . One could say that the courage to be is the courage to accept oneself as accepted in spite of being unacceptable . . . Accepting acceptance though being unacceptable is the basis for the courage of confidence.[13]

As so often Tillich's thinking is at its best not in doctrinal exposition but in sermons. This what he said from the pulpit:

> Grace strikes us when we are in great pain and restlessness . . . It strikes us when, year after year, the longed-for perfection of life does not appear, when the old compulsions reign within us, as they have for decades, when despair destroys all joy and courage. Sometimes at that moment a wave of light breaks into our darkness, and it is as though a voice were saying: "You are accepted. *You are accepted*, accepted by what which is greater than you . . . *Simply accept the fact that you are accepted*".[14]

I cite Tillich at length because this seems to me an admirable use of the scientific language of psychology to express a deep and profound truth about God's relationship to us in a way that is alive for us today.

With considerably more diffidence I put before you a modern symbol not taken from the human sciences but from electronics. It concerns the soul, which is not a very popular word today, but it is a concept which

13. P. Tillich, *Courage To Be*, (Nisbet, 1952), p.156.
14. P. Tillich, *The Shaking of the Foundations*, (SCM Press), p.161f.

Christians still need. We rightly scorn the idea that the soul is a ghost in a machine, the soul being the ghost and the machine being our body. We know that the human person is a unity. There is not one part of us which consists of our body and another separate part which consists of our soul. We are aware of the mystery of consciousness: we are conscious of our surroundings, of other people and of ourselves. Sometimes we are even conscious of God. But we cannot separate our consciousness from our brain.

At the same time we believe that after we die we shall be raised up to a new mode of existence. The body will be dead. We cannot imagine existing without a body, because it is through the body that we are in communication with others: a bare soul would be entirely passive and isolated. And so we believe that we shall be raised with a new body. What then is the element of continuity that ensures that it will be you and I that are raised, and not new people? We cannot believe that God will recreate our soul for the life to come, any more than we can believe that he will recreate our physical bodies. The element of continuity must be the soul.

It is traditional Christian belief, derived from St Thomas Aquinas, that the soul is the form of the body. The human soul enables the body to live, and gives it consciousness. So we form not a bare unity, but a duality, with body and soul joined together in the closest possible relationship. According to the traditional doctrine, the soul is real, it is substantial, and it can exist on its own, admittedly in an attenuated form, before being joined to another body.

While that is the traditional belief of Christians, I do not think that many Christians actually believe it any more, at least in that form. We have to admit that something rather like this traditional belief is required, if we are to retain our belief in resurrection, but we have no living experience which can act as a symbol for such a belief.

I would like to suggest the imagery of a word processor and a computer. It consists of both hardware and software. The hardware is an electronic machine, solid substance, wonderfully intricate, not unlike the body except that the hardware is a machine and our bodies are organisms. A word processor will not function without software. It is no use on its own. The software becomes temporarily *embodied* in the hardware. The software also is of no use on its own, except for storage. But when it is embodied in the hardware, it makes, as it were, the hardware come alive. What is more, my word processor is what is called compatible. The software may be used with other types of computer; and in the same way the soul, after this life, is embodied in a new and glorious body.

When I put this imagery before an academic audience not long ago, there were, as I should have foreseen, many objections. Computer software, I was told, is a material substance: the soul is immaterial. Of course it is spiritual substance. I was only suggesting an analogy. And again it was objected that software is manufactured, while the soul is mysteriously joined to the body, no one knows quite when. Of course it is. It seems to well up within the body as it develops from the one-celled fertilised egg that marks all human beginnings. I gladly admit all these and other deficiencies in the symbolism. No symbol perfectly represents that which it symbolises, but it can communicate a reality in a vivid way by means of another experienced reality. I give this analogy of hardware and software in a computer as an example of electronics helping to communicate the Christian gospel in a scientific age.

The general theme of all lectures given on the William Barclay foundation is the communication of the Gospel. I have been, in all three lectures, trying to examine what is meant by communication, and the difficulties and advantages of living in a scientific age for the communication of the Gospel. In the first lecture I tried to show the difference between the scientific attitude and the religious attitude, and what they have in common. It is important to remind ourselves that modern science began as it were under Christian auspices; and I gave some reasons to show why that was the case. I tried to show that modern science is not mechanistic as it was formerly believed to be. While there are some real problems from science for religion, I suggested to you that, contrary to popular belief science actually supports religion rather than opposes it.

It is hard to gain a hearing for faith when so many people think that science has shown it to be old-fashioned and out-dated. I tried to show that the tide has changed, and that this in turn has now become an old-fashioned view of the relation of science to religion. Indeed a study of the evolutionary process suggest that there is a point and purpose behind it.

In the second lecture I tried to show the illumination that modern knowledge of the human sciences as much as the natural sciences can bring to our understanding of the Gospel; and I glanced at scientific history and the sciences of literary and linguistic criticism. Turning to the natural sciences, I discussed some problems which religion poses for the sciences, including miracles, the Virginal Conception of Jesus and the Empty Tomb at his Resurrection; and I tried to show some ways through these problems. In this third lecture I have been considering the nature of communication, and I have been thinking about ways in which the sciences can actually help us in communicating the gospel in this scientific age.

You may think that in these lectures I have been unduly cerebral. I don't think that I know of anyone who became a Christian simply by taking thought. It was certainly not as a result of a cerebral process that I myself came to faith in God, but through my good fortune in having God-fearing parents who knew and loved God and who passed on their faith to me. Again, I did not myself come to faith in Jesus as Lord through studying the Gospel or through intellectual arguments, but as a result of a vivid and overwhelming personal experience which changed the course of my life. The reality of God often breaks into a person's life as a result of some joy or sorrow, or because of the impact of the character of some believing Christian. But God works in many ways, and all of us are different. We can set no bounds to the grace of God. He can bring into being possibilities of which we never dreamed. Faith cannot be manufactured for us by others, nor can we manufacture it for ourselves. Faith is a gift from God. This holds good for a scientific age or for any other kind of age we like to consider.

At the same time there are circumstances which make it easy to come to faith, and circumstances which make it difficult. Strangely enough, dangers and difficulties and discrimination against Christians are not obstacles for the communication of the Gospel. It almost seems to thrive on opposition; and, if we look at the history of the church down the ages, we have to admit the truth of that old saying of Tertullian that the blood of the martyrs is the seed of the church.

None of this however should preclude us from considering the implications of the sciences—both the human sciences and the natural sciences—for the communication of the Gospel. And this for several reasons. In the first place, we need to pursue truth wherever it may be found, because all truth comes from God, and through the sciences we gain deeper knowledge about the world in which God has set us. Secondly, we need to be able to rebut the false arguments of those who allege that the scientific attitude is absolutely opposed to religious attitudes, and that science has shown religion to be outmoded. There is nothing worse than to be thought outmoded. It is one thing to be opposed as pernicious—Christians are well used to that. But it is quite another to be ignored as being irrelevant; and this false idea is often put about in the mass media of communication.

Thirdly, in a scientific age we need to use scientific ideas in the communication of the Gospel; and finally we need to demonstrate, as I believe that we can, that the world of science actually requires a religious explanation for its own existence. In these ways we can recapture for the Gospel some of the high intellectual ground that it has lost, and by so doing we are better able to communicate its Good News to the millions in this land who neither know it nor accept it.

That is the challenge that lies before us.